MEL BAY PRESENTS
101 AMAZING JAZZ BASS PATTERNS

BY LARRY McCABE

BOOK CONTENTS

Introduction	2
How to Use This Book	3
Projects for Students	5
Major Patterns (C)	6
Dorian Patterns (Dm7)	8
Mixolydian Patterns (G7)	10
iim7-V7-I Patterns (Dm7-G7-C)	12
Modified iim7-V7-I Patterns	14
Four-Bar Patterns	17
Eight-Bar Patterns	23
Bridge Patterns	29
Turnarounds	34
Appendix 1. Basic Theory for the Jazz Musician	36
Appendix 2. Major Scales	44
Appendix 3. Dorian Scales	45
Appendix 4. Mixolydian Scales	46
Appendix 5. Moveable Scale Diagrams	47

CD CONTENTS

1 "E" tuning note [:40]	14 Ex. 25-26 [:28]	27 Ex. 51-52 [:36]	40 Ex. 77-78 [:52]
2 Ex. 1-2 [:24]	15 Ex. 27-28 [:28]	28 Ex. 53-54 [:37]	41 Ex. 79-80 [:52]
3 Ex. 3-4 [:29]	16 Ex. 29-30 [:36]	29 Ex. 55-56 [:38]	42 Ex. 81-82 [:50]
4 Ex. 5-6 [:32]	17 Ex. 31-32 [:39]	30 Ex. 57-58 [:35]	43 Ex. 83-84 [:52]
5 Ex. 7-8 [:34]	18 Ex. 33-34 [:28]	31 Ex. 59-60 [:38]	44 Ex. 85-86 [:53]
6 Ex. 9-10 [:26]	19 Ex. 35-36 [:31]	32 Ex. 61-62 [:39]	45 Ex. 87-88 [:52]
7 Ex. 11-12 [:27]	20 Ex. 37-38 [:28]	33 Ex. 63-64 [:38]	46 Ex. 89-90 [:52]
8 Ex. 13-14 [:30]	21 Ex. 39-40 [:30]	34 Ex. 65-66 [:35]	47 Ex. 91-92 [:40]
9 Ex. 15-16 [:31]	22 Ex. 41-42 [:28]	35 Ex. 67-68 [:36]	48 Ex. 93-94 [:32]
10 Ex. 17-18 [:29]	23 Ex. 43-44 [:31]	36 Ex. 69-70 [:50]	49 Ex. 95-96 [:34]
11 Ex. 19-20 [:29]	24 Ex. 45-46 [:33]	37 Ex. 71-72 [1:05]	50 Ex. 97-98 [:31]
12 Ex. 21-22 [:32]	25 Ex. 47-48 [:36]	38 Ex. 73-74 [1:00]	51 Ex. 99-100 [:32]
13 Ex. 23-24 [:31]	26 Ex. 49-50 [:37]	39 Ex. 75-76 [:54]	52 Ex. 101 [:25]

© 2000 BY MEL BAY PUBLICATIONS, INC., PACIFIC, MO 63069.
ALL RIGHTS RESERVED. INTERNATIONAL COPYRIGHT SECURED. B.M.I. MADE AND PRINTED IN U.S.A.
No part of this publication may be reproduced in whole or in part, or stored in a retrieval system, or transmitted in any form or by any means, electronic, mechanical, photocopy, recording, or otherwise, without written permission of the publisher.

Visit us on the Web at http://www.melbay.com — E-mail us at email@melbay.com

INTRODUCTION

This book/CD set teaches 101 jazz bass patterns played over chords and chord progressions that are basic in the harmonic language of jazz. If you currently play blues, country, folk, classical or rock, and desire to venture into jazz, this book is for you.

Because each pattern is played over a "real" chord progression, it will be easy for you to relate the examples to "real" music. In addition, you will experience noticeable improvement in your knowledge of the fingerboard, your technical facility, your harmonic vocabulary and your ability to conceive and express modern musical ideas.

I sincerely hope that this collection of *101 Amazing Jazz Bass Patterns* brings you much musical growth and personal satisfaction.

Larry McCabe
Tallahassee, Florida 1997

MEL BAY TITLES BY LARRY MCCABE
Títulos de Mel Bay por Larry McCabe

- Blues, Boogie, and Rock Guitar
- Blues Band Rhythm Guitar
- Country Lead Guitar
- You Can Teach Yourself™ Song Writing
- Anthology of American Rock and Roll Guitar Styles
- Anthology of American Rock and Roll Bass Styles
- 101 Blues Guitar Turnaround Licks
- 101 Nashville Style Guitar Licks
- 101 Blues Bass Patterns
- 101 Mississippi Delta Blues Fingerpicking Licks
- 101 Dynamite Rock Guitar Rhythm Patterns*
  101 magníficos patrones ritmicas de rock para guitarra*
- 101 Dynamite Rock Bass Patterns*
  101 magníficos patrones de rock para bajo*

- 101 Dynamite Latin Bass Patterns*
  101 magníficos patrones latinos para bajo*
- 101 Fingerstyle Guitar Accompaniment Patterns*
  101 patrones de acompañamiento de guitarra
  en el estilo de punteo con los dedos*
- 101 Dynamite Blues Guitar Fill-In Licks*
  101 maravillosos rellenos en el estilo de blues para guitarra*
- 101 Dynamite Rock Guitar Riffs*
  101 melodías cortas (*riffs*) para la guitarra en estilo de rock*
- 101 Dynamite Slide Guitar Licks in Open E Tuning*
  101 frases maravillosas para la guitarra deslizante (*slide*)
  afinando las cuerdas para sonar un acorde de mí*
- 101 *Red-Hot* Swing Guitar Licks
- 101 *Amazing* Jazz Bass Patterns

*Text in both English and Spanish   *Libros en inglés y español

CREDITS

Bass	Randy Barnhill
Guitars	Larry McCabe
Drawings	Steve McCabe
Recording Engineer	Fred Chester
Music Editor	Randy Barnhill

HOW TO USE THIS BOOK

The Written Music

1. Each musical example in this book is in the key of C major. This format provides a consistent point of reference (the key of C major) and facilitates ease in theoretical analysis and comparison of examples.

2. Each example is written in both notation and tablature exactly as it is recorded.

Fingerings

Suggested fretting-hand fingerings are provided in the notation staff. The recommended fingerings are not absolute, and you may modify a particular fingering if you have a better idea.

1 = First (index) finger   2 = Second (middle) finger   3 = Third (ring) finger   4 = Fourth (little) finger

Swing Eighths

For ease of reading, the eighth notes are written as "straight" (or "even") eighths. However, each pair of eighth notes actually sounds like the first and third note of an eighth-note triplet. This "swing" effect (a longer note followed by a shorter note) is a central component of jazz music.

If the concept of *swing eighths* is new to you, be sure to listen to some jazz recordings (or the companion CD) to absorb the feel of this rhythm.

Chord Symbols

Chord symbols are indicated above the music. The following remarks explain how chord symbols are interpreted by jazz musicians.

Major Chords

Because we rarely play a "plain" triad in jazz, a major chord symbol (such as C) does not necessarily limit you to the tones of the major triad. If your ear tells you that a C6 sounds better than a plain C triad, play the C6.

For example, The **C major** chord symbol (C) might be interpreted as any of the following: C6, C Major 7, C6/9, C add9, or any other chord in the C major family (see Appendix 1, Basic Theory for the Jazz Musician).

In jazz, this latitude of choice applies to all basic chord symbols.

Minor Chords

A minor chord symbol (such as Dm) does not necessarily limit you to the minor triad.

For example, the **D minor** chord symbol (Dm) might be interpreted as Dm6, Dm7, Dm9, Dm 6/9, Dm11, or any other chord in the D minor family.

Exception: The 9th tone is normally not used for a minor chord that functions as iiim (Ex: Em in the key of C; Am in the key of F).

Dominant Seventh Chords

The **G dominant seventh** chord symbol (G7) might be interpreted as G7/6, G9, G13, or any other chord in the G dominant family.

All chords–especially dominant chords–can also be *altered* (see below).

Embellished Chords, Extended Chords, and Altered Chords

1. Adding the 6th and/or 7th tone to a triad creates an *embellished* chord (C6, CMaj7, Dm7).

2. Adding a 9th, 11th, or 13th tone to a chord creates an *extended* chord (G9, G13). The 6th tone is called a 13th if there is also a 9th tone in the chord.

3. A chord may be *altered* by any of the following methods:

   a) Raise or lower the fifth tone by a half-step (G7♭5, G7♯5).

   b) Raise or lower the ninth tone by a half-step (G7♭9, G7♯9)

   c) Raise the eleventh (fourth) tone by a half-step (G7♯11).

4. In jazz, alterations are used for all types of chords, but they are most often applied to dominant chords. For example, the following altered chords are often used in place of G7:

G7♯5 (also written G7+5, or Gaug7); G7♭5; G7♯9; G7♭9; G7♯11.

5. A dominant seventh chord that functions as III7 (E7 in the key of C) usually has a flatted 9th tone (if the ninth tone is sounded).

6. A dominant seventh chord that functions as VI7 (A7 in the key of C) usually has a flatted 9th tone (if the ninth tone is sounded).

7. A dominant seventh chord usually has a flatted 9th tone (if the ninth tone is sounded) when moving to a minor chord whose root is a perfect fourth higher (E7 to Am7).

8. Major chords are sometimes altered by flatting the fifth (C7♭5).

9. A minor chord often has a flatted 5th (Dm7♭5), especially in a iim7-V7 progression (Dm7 to G7).

10. A seventh chord can be both extended and altered (G9♯5, Dm9♭5, etc.) at the same time.

Mel Bay's *Blues Band Rhythm Guitar* by Larry McCabe is a comprehensive book (150+ pages) that clearly explains chord embellishments, extensions, alterations, and substitutions.

Patterns 1-101

The 101 musical examples are divided into nine categories (see the Table of Contents). These categories include one-chord patterns as well as essential chord progressions of two to eight bars. Appendix 1, <u>Basic Theory For the Jazz Musician</u>, offers essential theoretical information relating to the nine categories of examples.

The Companion CD

1. Several "E" tuning notes are provided on the first track of the companion CD.

2. The CD, recorded in stereo, is mixed as follows: The drums and the rhythm guitar are in the <u>center</u>
The bass guitar is on the <u>left</u>
The lead guitar is on the <u>right</u>

3. If you wish, you may remove either the lead guitar or the bass by turning down the appropriate speaker.

4. Most of the examples are assigned an individual track. Because the current technology allows only 99 tracks, a few tracks contain two examples. For your convenience, we placed the turnarounds (which are short in duration) on these "doubled" tracks.

The guitar licks heard on the C.D. may be found in the companion book/CD set entitled *101 Red-Hot Swing Guitar Licks* (available from Mel Bay Publications).

Procedure

Although it might be easiest to start with the short patterns (1-24), you may work through the patterns in any order. If you encounter a pattern that is too difficult, try another pattern and return to the more challenging example later.

PROJECTS FOR STUDENTS

The following projects will benefit all students.

1. Transpose each pattern to every root tone and practice through the cycle of fourths:
C F B♭ E♭ A♭ D♭ G♭ B E A D G

2. Vary a pattern by changing the timing of one or more notes.

3. Play a pattern either one octave higher or lower than written, if possible.

4. Compose a variation on a pattern by substituting a new note for an existing note.

5. Study Appendix 1, "Basic Theory for the Jazz Musician."

6. Learn the scales in Appendices 2-4.

7. Try to learn several patterns by ear from the companion C.D.

8. Learn several patterns from the book without listening to the C.D.

9. Compose an original pattern to fit a given chord progression.

10. Find a dorian (Dm7) pattern that uses the natural fifth tone (A). Lower this note by one-half step to A♭. Determine whether this alteration is an improvement over the original pattern. (See **patterns 9-16.**)

11. Find a mixolydian (G7) pattern that uses the natural fifth tone (D). Lower this note by one-half step. Determine whether this alteration is an improvement over the original pattern. (See **patterns 17-24.**)

12. Find a mixolydian (G7) pattern that uses the natural ninth tone (A). Lower this note by one-half step. Determine whether this alteration is an improvement over the original pattern. (See **patterns 17-24.**)

If any of these concepts are unclear, see a good music teacher for guidance. If there is no one in your area who is professionally qualified to teach your instrument, study theory with a good teacher who plays a different instrument.

Major Patterns

Major Patterns . . . continued

Dorian Patterns

Dorian Patterns . . . continued

Mixolydian Patterns

Mixolydian Patterns . . . continued

iim7-V7-I Patterns

iim7-V7-I Patterns ... continued

Modified iim7-V7-I Patterns

Modified iim7-V7-I Patterns ... continued

Modified iim7-V7-I Patterns . . . continued

Four-Bar Patterns

Four-Bar Patterns . . . continued

Each example can be resolved to the tonic chord (C major). See Ex. 54-55 below.

Four-Bar Patterns ... continued

Four-Bar Patterns ... continued

Four-Bar Patterns . . . continued

Four-Bar Patterns . . . continued

See Mel Bay's *Anthology of American Rock and Roll Bass Styles* to learn how to play all the important rock bass styles.

Eight-Bar Patterns

Eight-Bar Patterns . . . continued

Eight-Bar Patterns ... continued

Eight-Bar Patterns ... continued

Eight-Bar Patterns . . . continued

Eight-Bar Patterns . . . continued

Bridge Patterns

Bridge Patterns . . . continued

Bridge Patterns . . . continued

Bridge Patterns ... continued

Bridge Patterns ... continued

Turnarounds

Turnarounds... continued

More turnarounds can be found in Mel Bay's *101 Blues Bass Patterns* by Larry McCabe.

Appendix 1
Basic Theory for the Jazz Musician

For the sake of uniformity and ease of analysis, all musical examples in this book are in the key of C major. For best results, transpose each example to all other major keys.

The terms *tone* and *note* are used interchangeably in the following discussion, as are the terms *song* and *tune*.

Scales
A musical *scale* is a series of several musical tones. Each *type* of scale is defined by: a) the number of notes in the scale, and b) the arrangement of the *intervals* of the scale (an interval is the distance between any two notes).

In Western music (European and American) the *major scale* is the most important scale. Example 1 shows the notes in the *C major scale* and the position of each note in the scale.

Example 1   The C major scale

1	2	3	4	5	6	7	8 (1)
C	D	E	F	G	A	B	C

The smallest interval (in Western music) is known as a *half-step*. On the piano, a half-step is the distance from one key to either of its neighboring keys. On the guitar, a half-step is the distance from one fret to either of its neighboring frets. Two half-steps make a *whole step*.

The major scale is constructed according to the following arrangement of half-steps (H) and whole steps (W): W-W-H-W-W-W-H.

There are 12 major scales in all, one for each musical tone. Scales are the foundation for *melody* (a tuneful arrangement of notes), *bass lines*, and *harmony* (a combining of 2 or more notes).

Tonic Note
The first note in a scale is called the *tonic* note (Ex. 2). This note functions as the "home" note of the scale or key (see below); that is, the tonic note provides a place of temporary or final resolution to a musical idea or composition.

Example 2   C is the tonic note in the C scale

1	2	3	4	5	6	7	8 (1)
C	D	E	F	G	A	B	C

Keys
Like a scale, a *key* is a series of tones related to a central tonic note. For instance, the C note is the tonic note in the *key of C major*. A key is similar to a scale in that a key is based on the tones of a corresponding scale. For example, a song in the key of C major uses the notes in the C major scale.

While a scale is comprised of <u>only</u> specific notes (the C major scale tones are C-D-E-F-G-A-B-C), a tune in a specific key can contain both scale tones and non-scale tones. For example, a song in the key of C major has as its foundation the C major scale tones, but it might also use one or more of the non-scale tones (D♭, E♭, G♭, A♭, B♭).

Diatonic and Non-Diatonic Notes
The notes of a particular scale (or key) are known as *diatonic* notes: the diatonic notes of the C major scale (and the key of C major) are shown in Ex. 1. A note that does not belong to a specific scale is called a *non diatonic* note. D♭, E♭, G♭, A♭, and B♭ are all non-diatonic notes in C major.

The simplest melodies use only diatonic (scale) notes. For example, "Twinkle, Twinkle, Little Star," played in the key of C, uses only the notes in the C scale. Performed in the key of G major, the song uses only the notes in the G scale. We would call "Twinkle" a diatonic song.

In contrast, more developed songs ("I Can't Give You Anything But Love") are spiced up with the use of non-diatonic notes. A developed melody often uses many non-diatonic notes, even though the song is still centered around the tonic note of the main scale.

Chords

Harmony is produced by the simultaneous sounding of two or more notes. A *chord* is a group of three or more musical tones sounded together.

There are several *types* of chords in music; our discussion begins with *major chords*. The most basic chord in the major chord family is the *major triad*. Each major triad is named by its fundamental tone; for example, the C major triad is known as C, the G major triad is called G, etc.

A major triad is constructed from the first, third, and fifth notes of its corresponding major scale. The C major triad (we usually just call it the C chord) contains the first, third, and fifth tones of the C scale (Ex. 3).

Example 3 The C chord

1	2	**3**	4	**5**	6	7	8 (1)
C	D	**E**	F	**G**	A	B	C

Formulas and Spellings

Each chord type (major, minor, etc.) is constructed according to a numerical *formula* which indicates the position of the chord tones in the major scale. The chord formula for the major triad is 1-3-5.

A specific chord formula is universal to all major scales. For example, the G major triad is made up of the 1-3-5 (the formula for the major triad) tones of the G scale (G-B-D).

Collectively, the tones in the chord are known as the *spelling*. The spelling of the C major triad is C-E-G; the G major triad is spelled G-B-D.

Tonic Chord

The tonic note acts as the central note of a specific scale or key. Similarly, the *tonic chord* functions as the "home" chord. The C major chord (C) is the *tonic* chord in the key of C.

As a rule, most songs end on the tonic chord. Along with the tonic note, the tonic chord provides a sense of resolution to a musical phrase or composition.

The tonic chord is also known as the *I chord*, with the numeral I indicating the position of the *fundamental* (or *root*) tone of the chord in the corresponding scale or key. Thus, C is the I chord in the key of C, G is the I chord in the key of G, and so on.

Although many songs end on the root of the tonic chord, the last note may also be either the third or the fifth tone of the tonic chord. In other words, songs in the key of C major will usually end on a C major chord played over a final melody note that is either C (1), E (3), or G (5). In most songs the tonic note is also the final bass note.

Diatonic and Non-Diatonic Chords

A chord composed only of notes from a specific scale (or key) is called a *diatonic chord*. The C chord is a diatonic chord in the key of C because all of its tones are found in the C scale. Conversely, a *non-diatonic chord* contains one or more tones not belonging to a particular scale or key. For example, an E major chord (E-G♯-B) is non-diatonic in the key of C because it contains a tone (G♯) that is not in the C scale.

Arpeggios (Broken Chords)

A series of chord tones played individually is known as an *arpeggio* or *broken chord*. When a musician plays the notes C–E–G–E in succession, (s)he is arpeggiating the C chord. Can you play the C chord tones on your instrument?

Major Chords

Each chord *family* (or type) contains a number of closely related chords. Example 4 lists several C major chords by name, formula and spelling.

Example 4 Basic C major chords

C	1-3-5	C–E–G
C6	1-3-5-6	C–E–G–A
CMaj7 (C Major 7)	1-3-5-7	C–E–G–B
C add 9	1-3-5-9	C–E–G–D
C6/9	1-3-5-6-9	C–E–G–A–D
CMaj9 (C Major 9)	1-3-5-7-9	C–E–G–B–D

The chords within a chord family are theoretically interchangeable. For instance, if the sheet music says C, it might be O.K. to substitute for C another chord in the C major family, such as C6 or CMaj7. Additionally, a bass player might play the notes C–E–G–A (C6) to a C chord–if the C6 arpeggio seems to support the particular musical context.

If some of the C major chords (Ex. 4) are new to you, you can learn their sound by playing the notes of each chord on either your instrument or the piano.

Patterns 1-8 in this book are played to the C (I) major chord. Each pattern should be transposed and played in all other major keys.

Extending the Scale

The 9th scale tone is used in three of the major chord formulas in Ex. 4. Chords that use the tones 9, 11, and 13 are called *extended chords*. The tones 9, 11, and 13 are found in the *extended scale* (Ex. 5).

Example 5   The C scale extended to the thirteenth

1	2	3	4	5	6	7	8 (1)	9	10	11	12	13
C	D	E	F	G	A	B	C	D	E	F	G	A

Scale/Chord Relationships

The scale that generates the tones of a particular chord is the "basic" scale for that chord. For example, the C major scale is the basic scale for the melodies, harmonies and bass lines that are played to C major chords in the key of C.

The Dorian Scale (Dorian Mode)

The *dorian scale* (also called the *dorian mode*) is another important scale in jazz music. The *D dorian scale* is shown in Ex. 6.

Example 6   The D dorian scale

1	2	3	4	5	6	7	8 (1)
D	E	F	G	A	B	C	D

The dorian scale is constructed according to the following arrangement of half-steps and whole steps: W-H-W-W-W-H-W. Can you play a D dorian scale on your instrument?

There are 12 dorian scales in all, one for each musical note. A dorian scale can be thought of as a "scale within a scale" (the term *mode* is often used to describe such scales). For example, D dorian is a reordering of the C major scale from the second tone, D.

If the C major and D dorian scales use the same notes, what makes the dorian different from the major? Quite simply, the particular construction of each scale gives that scale a unique sound.

A dorian scale has as its tonic the second tone of its "parent" major scale. Put a different way, the tonic of a dorian scale is a whole step above the tonic of its "parent" major scale. Hence, D dorian has the same notes as C major, E dorian has the same notes as D major, and so on.

It is also possible to construct a dorian scale by lowering both the third and seventh tones of a major scale by a half-step (Ex. 7).

Example 7   The C dorian scale (parent scale: Bb major)

1	2	b3	4	5	6	b7	8 (1)
C	D	Eb	F	G	A	Bb	C

The dorian scale is a *minor scale*. There are a number of different types of minor scales, and they all have one thing in common: a flatted third tone (b3). In addition, all minor scales–with the exception of the *harmonic minor scale* –also contain a flatted seventh tone (b7). A flatted third (also called a *minor third*) is a third major scale tone lowered by a half-step; a flatted seventh (also called a *minor seventh*) is a seventh major scale tone lowered by a half-step.

The dorian scale is the basic scale for the iim7 chord (see below).

The iim7 Chord

The iim7 chord (Dm7 in the key of C) is another important chord in jazz music. Example 8 shows the name, formula and spelling for several D minor chords.

Example 8   Basic D minor chords

Dm	1–b3–5	D–F–A
Dm6	1–b3–5–6	D–F–A–B
Dm7	1–b3–5–b7	D–F–A–C
Dm9	1–b3–5–b7–9	D–F–A–C–E
Dm6/9	1–b3–5–6–9	D–F–A–B–E
Dm11	1–b3–5–b7–11	D–F–A–C–G

Like minor scales, all minor chords contain a flatted third tone. In addition, the seventh tone (when there is one) is flatted in all minor chords except for the *minorMaj7* chord.

The basic scale for a iim7 chord is the corresponding dorian scale (Ex. 9): The notes in Dm7 (and many other Dm chords) are found in the D Dorian scale.

Example 9   Dm7 is generated by D dorian

D   E   F   G   A   B   C   D

Patterns 9-16 are played to the Dm7 (iim7) chord. Each pattern should be transposed and played in all major keys.

The Mixolydian Scale (Mixolydian Mode)

The *mixolydian scale* (or mode) is, along with the major and dorian scales, one of the "big three" basic scales in jazz music. The *G mixolydian scale* is shown in Ex. 10.

Example 10   The G mixolydian scale

1	2	3	4	5	6	7	8 (1)
G	A	B	C	D	E	F	G

The construction of the mixolydian scale is W-W-H-W-W-H-W. Can you play a G mixolydian scale on your instrument?

There are 12 mixolydian scales, one for each musical note. Like the dorian scale, a mixolydian scale is a mode, or a "scale within a scale." For instance, G mixolydian is a reordering of the C major scale from its fifth tone (G).

Each mixolydian scale has as its tonic the fifth tone of its "parent" major scale. Put a different way, the tonic of a mixolydian scale is 3 1/2 steps (a *perfect fifth*) above the tonic of its "parent" major scale. Therefore, G mixolydian is generated by C major, A mixolydian is generated by D major, and so on.

It is also possible to construct a mixolydian scale by lowering the seventh tone of a major scale by a half-step (Ex.11).

Example 11   The C mixolydian scale (parent scale: F major)

1	2	3	4	5	6	b7	8 (1)
C	D	E	F	G	A	Bb	C

The mixolydian scale is a *dominant scale*. Dominant scales, which contain both a natural third and a flatted seventh, are built on the fifth degree of the major scale. The mixolydian scale is the basic scale for the V7 chord (see below).

The V7 chord

Next to the tonic chord, the *V7 chord* is the most important chord in Western music. The V7 chord creates tension that seeks resolution to the tonic (I) chord. G7, the V7 chord in the key of C, sounds like it wants to move to the C chord.

Built on the fifth degree of the scale, the V7 chord is the basic chord in the *dominant chord* family. A *dominant chord* symbol consists of the name of a musical tone followed by the number 7, 9, 11 or 13 (G7, G9, etc.).

Because the basic dominant chord is a four-note *dominant seventh chord* (G7, D7, etc.), some musicians loosely refer to dominant chords as "seventh chords." Example 12 shows the name, formula and spelling for several G dominant chords.

Example 12   Basic G dominant chords

G7	1-3-5-♭7	G–B–D–F
G7/6	1-3-5-6-♭7	G–B–D–E–F
G9	1-3-5-♭7-9	G–B–D–F–A
G13*	1-3-5-♭7-9-13	G–B–D–F–A–E

* The sixth tone is called the thirteenth if there is also both a seventh and a ninth tone in the chord.

As shown in Ex. 12, the formula for the basic dominant chord–the dominant seventh–is 1-3-5-♭7. In regards to G7, the 1-3-5-♭7 formula indicates the first (G), third (B), fifth (D), and flatted seventh (F) tones of the G major scale. Like dominant scales, all dominant chords contain both a natural third and a flatted seventh. (A major scale contains a natural third and a natural seventh; a minor scale contains a flatted third and–with the exception of the *harmonic minor scale*–a flatted seventh.)

The basic scale for a V7 chord is the corresponding mixolydian scale (Ex. 13).

Example 13   G7 is generated by G mixolydian

G   A   B   C   D   E   F   G

Patterns 17-24 are played to the G7 (V7) chord. Each pattern should be transposed and played in all other major keys.

The iim7-V7-I Chord Progression

The *iim7-V7-I progression* is the most important chord progression in jazz. In the key of C, the iim7-V7-I progression is Dm7-G7-C. Example 14 shows several typical iim-V7-I progressions in the key of C major.

In the key of C, V7 can be understood to mean any chord in the G dominant family, iim7 can be understood to be any chord in the D minor family (except for the DmMaj7 chord), and I can be taken to mean any chord in the C major family.

Example 14   Various iim-V7-I chord progressions in C major

1. **Dm7-G7-C**
2. **Dm7-G7-C6**
3. **Dm7-G9-Cmaj7**
4. **Dm9-G13-C6/9**
5. **Dm11-G9-Cmaj9**

Notice that the root tones move in ascending *perfect fourths* (a perfect fourth is an interval of 2 1/2 steps) in the iim7-V7-I chord progression.

Patterns 25-32 are played to the iim7-V7-I chord progression in the key of C. Each pattern should be transposed and played in all other major keys.

Modified iim7-V7-I Chord Progressions

It is possible to modify a iim7-V7-I chord progression by *substituting* other chords for iim7 and/or V7 (Ex. 15). Chord substitutions provide variety and, often, a more "jazzy" sound.

Example 15   Substitutions for iim7 and V7

   1. **Substitute ♭VI7 (A♭7) for iim7 (Dm7).**

Principle: Substitute for the iim7 chord the dominant chord that is built on the flatted sixth tone of the tonic major scale.

   2. **Substitute ♭II7 (D♭7) for V7 (G7).**

Principle: Substitute for the V7 chord the dominant chord that is built on the flatted second tone of the tonic major scale.

Patterns 33-47 are played to *modified iim7-V7-I progressions* in C major. Transpose and play each pattern in all major keys.

Altered Chords

An *altered chord* is a chord with one or more of the following altered scale tones: ♭5, ♯5, ♭9, ♯9, ♯11, ♭6 (♭13). Because an altered chord contains at least one non-diatonic tone, it sounds more modern ("jazzy") than a plain unaltered chord.

Along with the iim7-V7-I chord progression, altered chords are a key element of jazz harmony. Several common altered chords are listed in Ex. 16.

Example 16 Altered chords

Example	Formula	Spelling
(Altered minor chords)		
Dm7♭5	1-♭3-♭5-♭7	D-F-A♭-C
Dm9♭5	1-♭3-♭5-♭7-9	D-F-A♭-C-E
Dm7♭6	1-♭3-♭5-♭6-♭7	D-F-A-B♭-C
(Altered dominant chords)		
G7♭5	1-3-♭5-♭7	G-B-D♭-F
G7♯5*	1-3-♯5-♭7	G-B-D♯-F
G7♭9	1-3-5-♭7-♭9	G-B-D-F-Ab
G7♯9	1-3-5-♭7-♯9	G-B-D-F-A♯
G7♯11	1-3-5-♭7-9-♯11	G-B-D-F-A-C♯
(Altered major chords)		
Cmaj7♭5	1-3-♭5-7	C-E-G♭-B
Cmaj7♯5	1-3-♯5-7	C-E-G♯-B

*The 7♯5 chord is also called 7aug5 (G7aug5), G7+, and G7+5.

Four-Bar Patterns

The four bar patterns in this book (**patterns 48-69**), set in the key of C, are played to common harmonic progressions that are found in thousands of songs. After learning these patterns, transpose each example to all other major keys.

Cycle of Fourths Progressions

Many of the patterns in this book are played to *cycle of fourths* chord progressions (for example, Em7-A7-Dm7-G7-C6). In a cycle of fourths progression, the chord root moves in perfect fourths through a chain of several chords.

The iim7-V7-I progression is perhaps the most common cycle of fourths progression.

Eight-Bar Patterns

Patterns 70-81 are played to standard eight-bar chord progressions in C. Some of these eight-bar progressions can be "complete" chord progressions for eight-bar tunes. For example, pattern 71 is played to a chord progression used for many 8-bar blues tunes such as "Trouble in Mind." (Ex. 17).

Example 17 A typical 8-bar chord progression

‖ I / / / | I7 / / / | IV / / / | ♯IVdim7 / / / | I / VI7 / | II7 / V7 / | I / IV / | I / / / ‖

The eight-bar progressions are also used for the "A" sections in AABA songs (see below).

AABA songs

The *AABA song form* is, along with the 12-bar blues, the most common song form in jazz. Example 18 shows how an AABA song is constructed. Can you rewrite this progression in Roman Numerals and transpose it to several other keys?

Example 18 A typical AABA song

A	‖ C / / /	C7 / / /	F / / /	D7 / / /	G7 / / /	Dm7 / G7 /	C / F /	C / / / ‖
A	‖ C / / /	C7 / / /	F / / /	D7 / / /	G7 / / /	Dm7 / G7 /	C / F /	C / / / ‖
B	‖ F / / /	F / F♯dim7 /	C / G7 /	C / Am7 /	D7 / / /	D7 / / /	G7 / / /	G7 / / / ‖
A	‖ C / / /	C7 / / /	F / / /	D7 / / /	G7 / / /	Dm7 / G7 /	C / F /	C / / / ‖

Many of the great *standard* songs in the jazz repertoire ("Stardust," "Georgia on My Mind," "Misty") are AABA songs. Usually 32 bars in length (four 8-bar sections), an AABA song is played as follows:

    1) The opening section is called the A section.
    2) Next, the A section is repeated to create an impression of familiarity in the mind of the listener.
    3) A contrasting section called the B section (the *bridge*) is played next. In music (as in life), variation is essential as too much repetition causes boredom.
    4) The A section is reprised for the final 8 bars.

In Ex. 18, each of the A sections is based on the chord progression for pattern 70, while the B section (the bridge) is based on the chord progression for pattern 86.

Bridges

Patterns 82-91 are played to standard 8-bar *bridge progressions* in C major. The competent musician must be well versed in these progressions as they are played in many songs.

You can study the AABA form by creating some "original" AABA chord progressions from the chord progressions this book. For the A sections, use the chords from one of the eight-bar patterns in this book (70-81). Use the same progression for all three A sections. For the B section, use the chords from one of the bridge patterns (82-91).

The chord progressions for each of the sections cannot be combined haphazardly, of course. The A and B parts must connect seamlessly in a way that makes musical sense.

Turnarounds

The term *turnaround* refers to a succession of chords (Ex. 19) played in the last two bars of a chord progression (or the last two bars of a section of a song). For example, a turnaround is often found in bars 7-8, 15-16, 23-24, and 31-32 of a 32-bar AABA song; bars 11-12 of a 12-bar blues; and in the final two bars of <u>any</u> song section.

Example 19 Two basic turnaround progressions

The most basic turnaround: || I / IV / | I / V7 / ||
Another common turnaround: || I / vim7 / | iim7 / V7 / ||

The turnaround helps to relieve the static harmony of playing only the tonic chord at the end of a section. Most turnarounds create tension that is relieved by resolution to the tonic chord.

The turnaround progressions in this book (**patterns 92-101**, played in C major) are essential to every musician's vocabulary. Try to apply some of the turnarounds to standard tunes (you will probably need to transpose, of course). In addition, create at least one original pattern to play with each turnaround chord progression.

Chord Tones, Scales, and Combination Patterns

For the most part, this book covers three types of musical patterns: 1) the chord tone method; 2) the scale tone method; 3) the combination method.

1. *The chord tone method* (also called the *arpeggio method*). Here, only the tones of the <u>chord of the moment</u> are used in the pattern. For example, the notes C (1) - E (3) - G (5) would be played to the C major chord. The 6th, 7th and 9th tones can also be used for a major chord; see Ex. 4 above.

Generally speaking, this method works best when the chords change frequently (every two beats). Caution must be exercised to prevent arpeggio playing from sounding like a technical exercise.

Another name for the chord tone method is *vertical* playing. The theme (head) to Benny Goodman's "Wholly Cats" is based exclusively on chord tones.

2) *The scale tone* (or *scalar*) *method*. This manner of playing utilizes uses all the notes in the scale that generates the chord(s) . For instance, the D dorian scale (Ex. 6) is played to Dm7, the G mixolydian scale (Ex. 10) is played to G7, and the C major scale (Ex. 1) is played to the C chord.

The scale tone method is also called *horizontal* playing. As a rule, the predominant use of the scalar method is best used with tunes with sparse chord changes. An example of such a tune is Herbie Hancock's "Maiden Voyage," a 32-bar AABA tune that has only four chords.

3) *Combination patterns.* For the sake of variety, most musicians use a combination of chord tones and scales in their playing.

Jazz Scales and Arpeggios

It is beyond the scope of this text to discuss the full range of scales employed by the jazz musician. However, the following tips should prove helpful:

1) When the chord symbol contains one or more altered tones, be sure to apply the altered tone(s) to the arpeggio or scale. For example, the arpeggio for G7♭5 would contain the notes G-B-**D**♭-F, and the G mixolydian scale for this chord would be modified to accommodate the flatted fifth tone (G-A-B-C-**D**♭-E-F-G).

2) A jazz musician will often "superimpose" an altered arpeggio (or scale) on a "plain" chord. For example, the sheet music might call for a G7 chord, but the musician will play a G7♭9 arpeggio (or another altered arpeggio or scale) because s/he finds it suitable to the musical context.

As you work through the musical examples in this book, be sure to analyze each pattern for the use of scale tones, chord tones and altered tones.

For Further Study

You Can Teach Yourself ® *Songwriting* by Larry McCabe contains many excellent entry-level and early intermediate theory lessons on song form, chord progressions, copyright and related subjects. The companion 92-track CD features a wealth of songs and helpful musical examples.

Blues Band Rhythm Guitar by Larry McCabe is a comprehensive 165-page book that covers chord embellishment, chord extension and chord substitution. The theoretical concepts taught in this book apply to all modern musical styles. A companion recording with 52 songs and musical examples is available.

Guitar players can learn many chords with the help of Mel Bay's *Deluxe Guitar Chord Encyclopedia*.

Bass players will find Mel Bay's *Deluxe Bass Chords, Arpeggios and Scales* to be an indispensible reference tool.

Each of the above books is published by Mel Bay Publications. In addition, a great variety of licks, rhythm patterns, and bass lines are found in Mel Bay's extensive *101 . . .* series of bass and guitar books by Larry McCabe.

Appendix 2
Major Scales

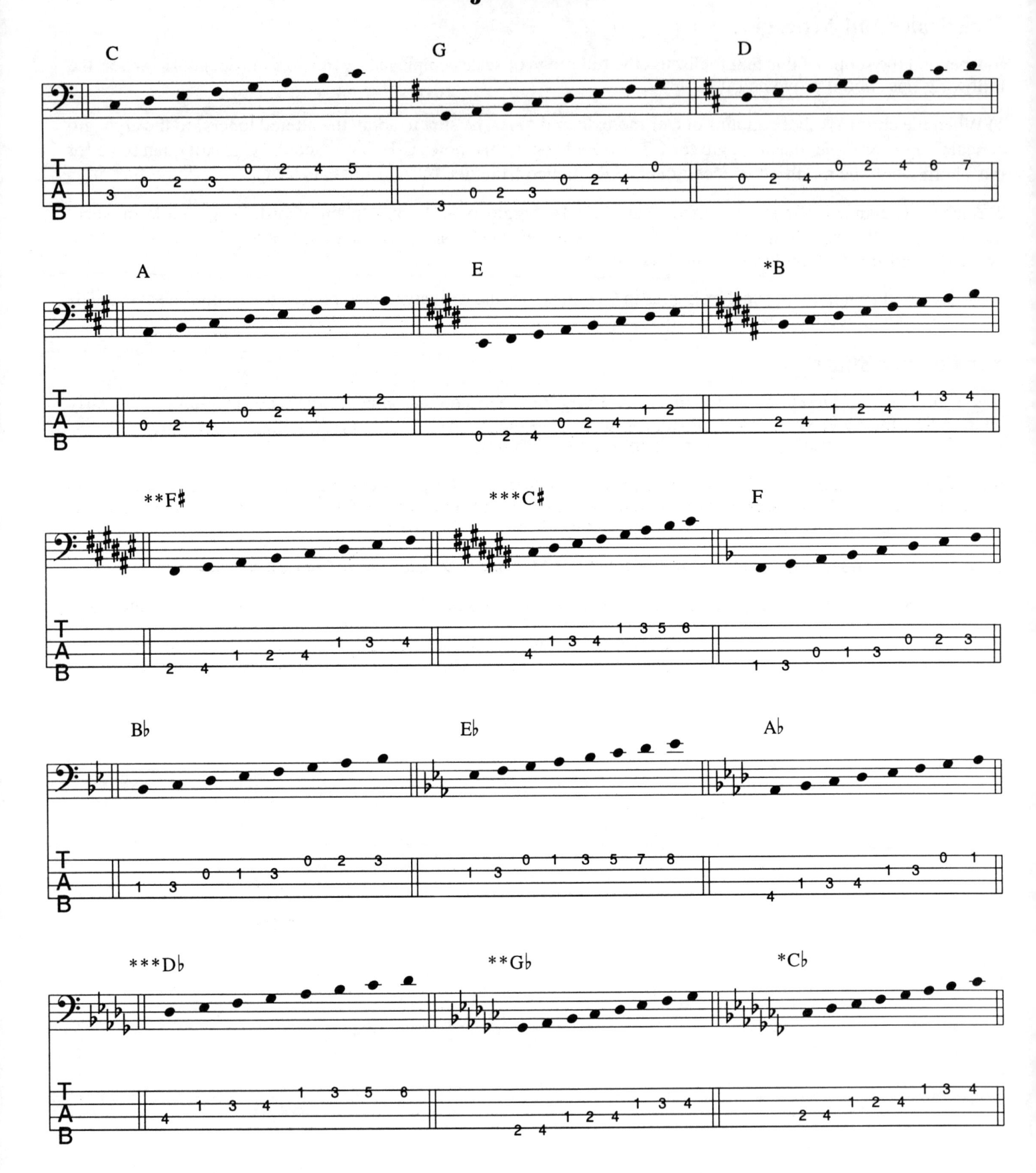

*Asterisks indicate enharmonic equivalent scales.

Appendix 3
Dorian Scales

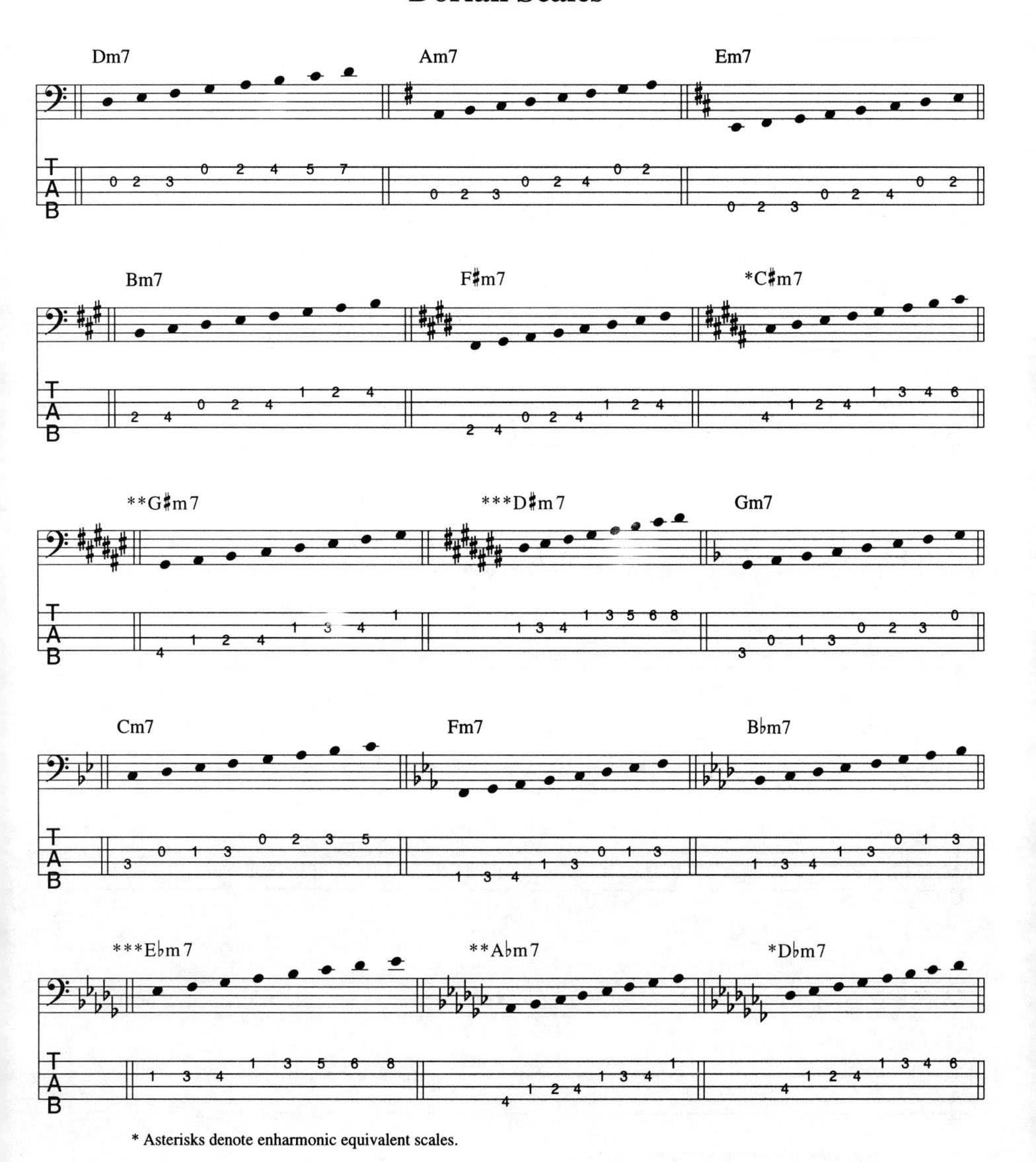

*Asterisks denote enharmonic equivalent scales.

Appendix 4
Mixolydian Scales

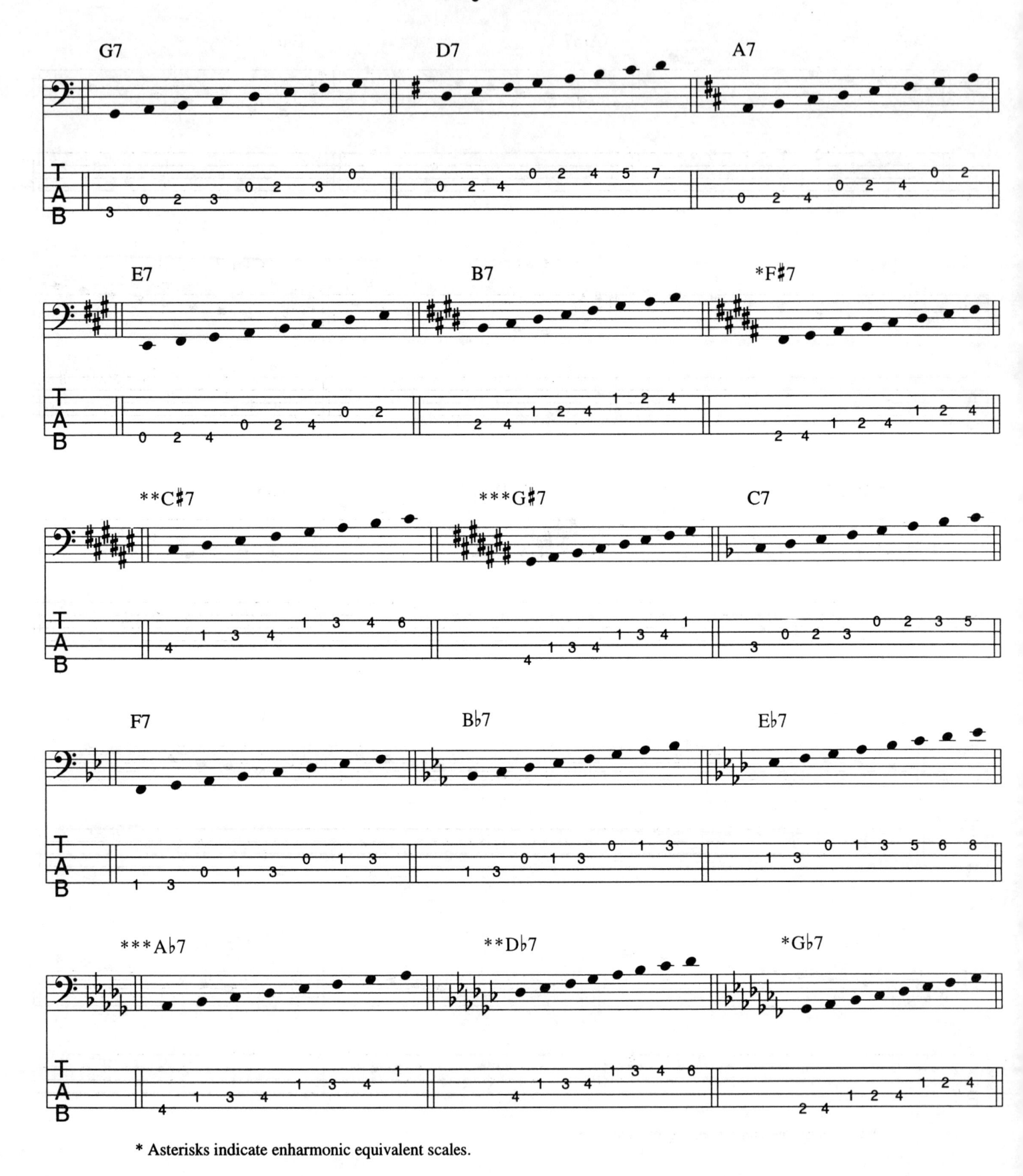

* Asterisks indicate enharmonic equivalent scales.

Appendix 5
Moveable Scales

● Root tone

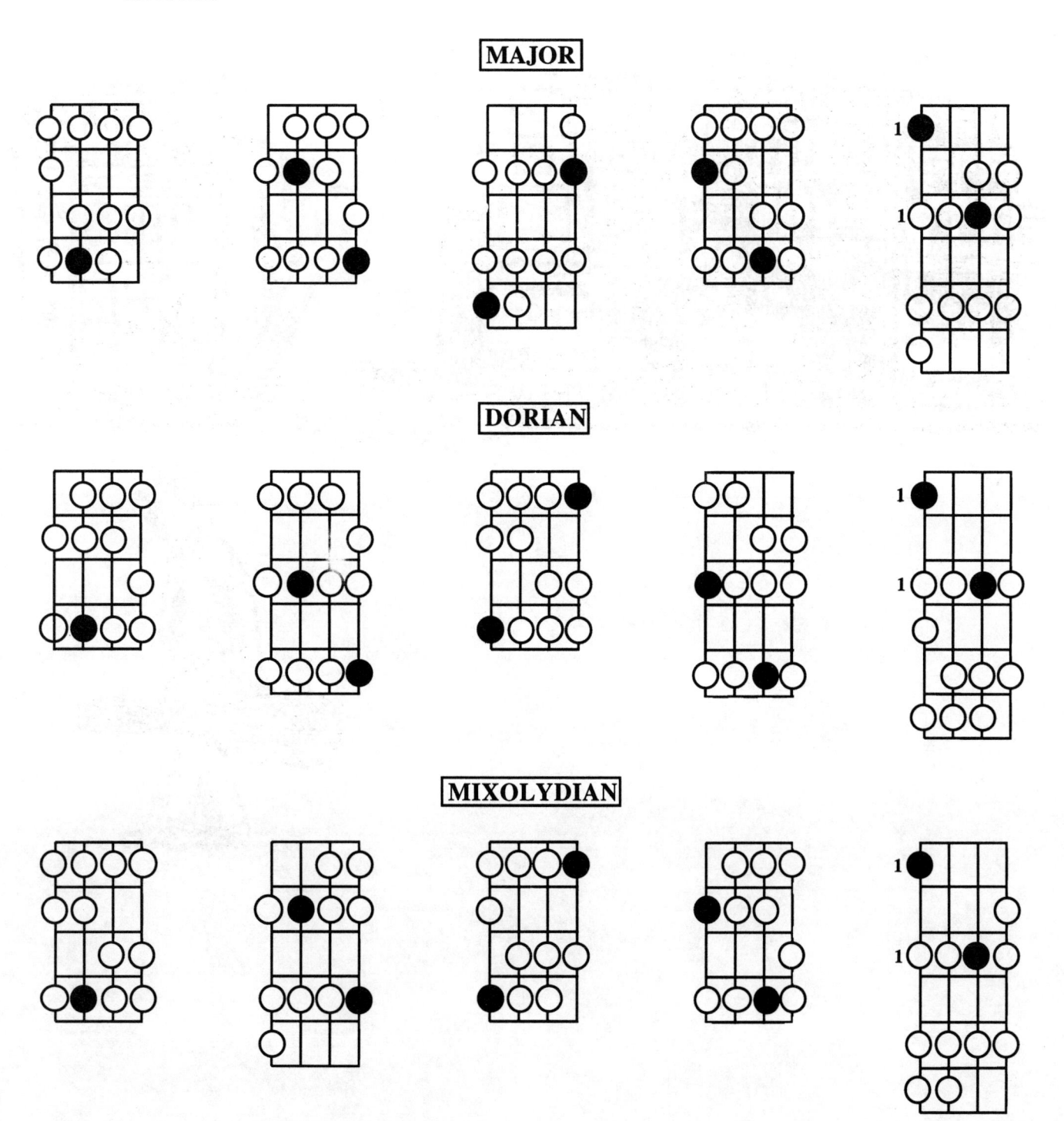

MAJOR

DORIAN

MIXOLYDIAN

47

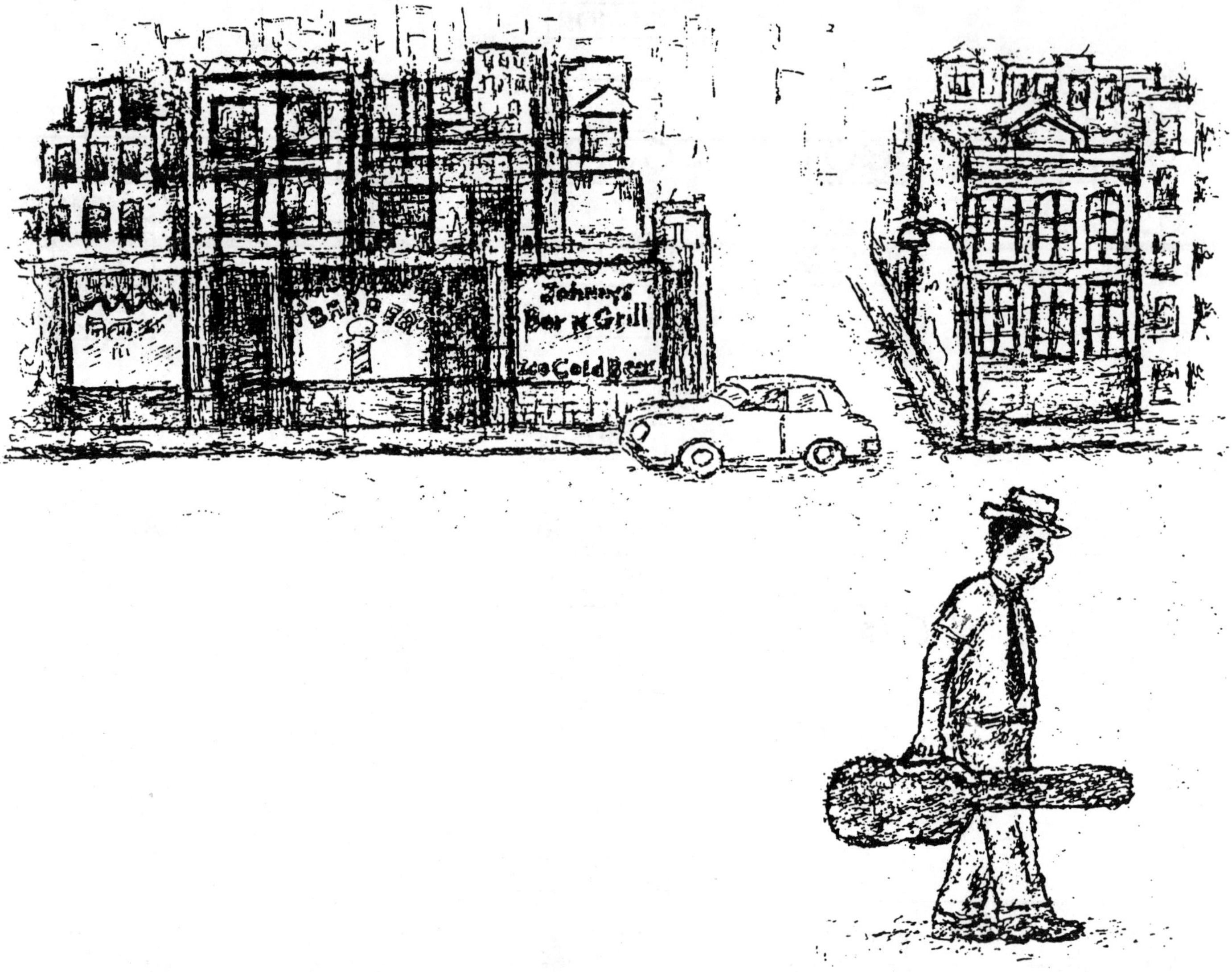
BARBER
Johnny's
Bar n Grill
Ice Cold Beer